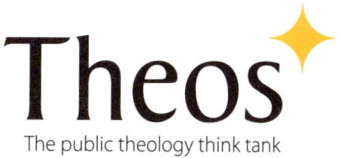

what Theos is

Theos is a public theology think tank which exists to undertake research and provide commentary on social and political arrangements. The word, "Theos", and our descriptor, "the public theology think tank", reflect our overall aim of putting God "back" into the public domain. Theos is about social, public theology; about public wisdom.

what Theos stands for

Faith is on the public agenda in a way that is unprecedented in recent times. Theos aims to shape events, not simply react to them. Our aim is to speak wisdom into the increasingly crowded market place of ideas. We seek to demonstrate that religion can have a positive role to play in public debate and the communities we seek to serve.

what Theos works on

Theos undertakes research on a wide range of subject areas. We believe that every issue is a moral issue and reject notions of a sacred/secular divide.

what Theos provides

Theos provides:

- high-quality research, reports and publications;
- an events' programme (including public debates, an annual Theos lecture and an extensive fringe programme at the party conferences);
- news, information and analysis to media companies and other opinion-formers, with a one-stop information line available to journalists; and
- an informative website, www.theosthinktank.co.uk

In addition to our independently driven work, Theos provides research, analysis and advice to individuals and organisations across the private, public and not-for-profit sectors. Our unique position within the think tank sector means that we have the capacity to develop proposals that carry values - with an eye to demonstrating what really works. Our staff and consultants have strong public affairs experience, an excellent research track record and a high level of theological literacy. We are practised in campaigning, media relations, detailed policy development and effecting policy change.

www.theosthinktank.co.uk

Published by Theos in 2007
© Theos

ISBN: 978-0-9554453-1-6

Some rights reserved – see copyright licence for details

For further information and subscription details please contact:

Theos
Licence Department
34 Buckingham Palace Road
London
SW1W 0RE
United Kingdom

T 020 7828 7777
E hello@theosthinktank.co.uk
www.theosthinktank.co.uk

Coming off the bench

The past, present and future of religious representation in the House of Lords

by Andrew Partington and Paul Bickley

contents

acknowledgements — 9

foreword — 10

introduction - Lords Spiritual — 13

chapter 1 - do bishops attend? — 26

chapter 2 - do bishops vote? — 31

chapter 3 - do bishops speak? — 36

chapter 4 - what do bishops say? — 40

chapter 5 - coming off the bench — 44

bibliography — 53

acknowledgements

The authors would like to thank all those who have assisted us during the course of the research, especially those who have consented to be interviewed for the work. Our interpretation and analysis of their submissions is exactly that.

We are also extremely grateful to those who have spent time reviewing the research, suggesting changes and developments to various drafts of the text and assisting in the production of the report itself.

foreword

In October 2006 the House of Commons' working party on House of Lords' Reform latest proposals were leaked to the press. The document emphasized the need to develop a cross-party consensus around a partly-appointed, partly-elected House, while maintaining the primacy of the House of Commons, and included proposals to abolish the remaining hereditary seats in the Lords, and cut the overall size of the House by one third. The leaked memorandum argued that the primary criteria for reform would be complementarity to the House of Commons.

On the subject of the religious representation in the House of Lords, the paper read:

> It is important that faith communities are formally represented in the House of Lords. The Church of England, as the established church, enjoys special status in the social and political life in England and more widely around the United Kingdom… Bishops have sat in the Lords since its inception…
>
> Furthermore, assuming the overall size of the House reduces, it would be difficult to justify retaining the current number of 26 Bishops. A practical solution would be to reduce the number of reserved places say from 26 to 16. This was proposed as long ago as 1968 and was at that time acceptable to the Church of England.
>
> It is equally important that a reformed House of Lords reflects the religious make up of the UK, even though it may be the case that not all individuals will be able to act as formal spokespersons for these particular faiths or beliefs … a duty could be placed on the Appointments Commission … to ensure that most major faiths together with those with no faith are represented in the House of Lords.

Twitchy secularists will be alarmed, and perhaps disappointed that an opportunity is being missed to finally and conclusively banish what they see as the anachronistic vestiges of religion in the public square. There will also be voices from the radical Christian traditions who will be equally concerned that the Christian community will continue to be contaminated with the exercise and legitimation of political authority. Notably, the document assumes a principle of diverse religious representation in the second chamber. This approach, although superficially unremarkable, has never before been adopted for, say, dissenting Christian traditions.

It may seem to some that the role of the religious representation in a reformed House is an uninteresting subcategory of a dry and dusty debate on stalled and politically unimportant constitutional reform. There may, indeed, be bigger fish to fry, but cynics should consider the increasing importance of the House of Lords, which is steering a largely politically independent course and has recently forced notable rethinks on a number of hastily conceived items of legislation, particularly in the arena of civil liberties. The question of religious representation is clearly one of significant importance: inclusion of other faith communities will institutionalize their perspectives, if only to a limited degree. It will signal their importance in public discourse and identify them with the political community in a new way. Indeed, it may establish religious diversity. Put another way, religious membership of the House of Lords is one factor in meeting one of the most intimidating challenges that we face as a society - that of managing a culturally and religiously plural public space.

This report takes a practical approach to the role of the bishops in a reformed second chamber, looking to analyse what they actually do, how they operate, what the barriers are to their fuller participation, and how the question of broader faith representation will alter the terms of debate. It outlines the historical and constitutional background of the Church of England's formal participation in the House of Lords, before setting out some statistical markers against the bishops' record under both Margaret Thatcher and Tony Blair. These findings will prompt pause for thought as we consider the impact of the increasing importance of faith and religion in our political institutions. Indeed, they indicate some politicization on the part of the bishops.

The report is not a dogmatic defence of the status quo, nor does it lurch confusedly from the clear imperfections of the existing system of religious representation to the zero sum game of aggressively secularizing political institutions. I hope that this piece of work and its findings will generate a full debate around the role of faith in a reformed second chamber.

Paul Woolley
Director, Theos
February 2007

introduction - Lords Spiritual

When the historian, David Starkey, recently compared the place of Church of England bishops in the House of Lords to that of religious leaders in Iran, and called the prospect of diverse religious representation in a reformed second chamber "grotesque", he probably reflected a degree of public confusion (and secularist consternation) around the role of the Lords Spiritual in Parliament.[1] Their presence, however, should not be dismissed, as is so often the case, as a hangover from mediaeval ecclesial power. That their presence is anachronistic is an easy accusation, but one which fails to take account of the (seemingly increasing) importance of faith in society or the complex historical development and constitutional subtleties of their role. The bishops are eligible to sit in the House of Lords as individual Lords of Parliament, but not peers, for peers could take part in the "judgements of blood" from which bishops were excluded by canon law.[2] Nor, strictly speaking, are the bishops present in the Upper House as corporate representatives of the Church of England. Hugh Montefiore, formerly Bishop of Birmingham, states it plainly:

> [Y]ou see, you're not there in the House of Lords as a representative of the Church. It's a very important point... you are not chosen to go to the House of Lords because you are a representative. You go in your own right as a bishop, a rather important distinction.[3]

It is equally important to note that the presence of the bishops in the House of Lords is not a factor of establishment. The Wakeham Commission Report on the Reform of the House of Lords was unequivocal in its assertion that "...there is no direct or logical connection between the establishment of the Church of England and the presence of the Church of England bishops in the second chamber".[4] The Church of Scotland, while established, has no representation in the House of Lords.

Michael L Nash reminds us that Edward I's Model Parliament, predating the establishment of the Church of England, incorporated 70 abbots, primarily in view of their status as literate landowners responsible for such hospitals, relief of the poor and such education as was available. He also notes that by the end of Edward II's reign in 1327 their numbers had already fallen to 27, and in fact that "most abbots were constantly seeking to be excused from distracting duties of state"[5] - a characteristic which has by no means disappeared completely from the bishops' approach. Wakeham provides a succinct summary of the historical development of episcopal representation in the Lords:

The origins of the bishops' role as members of the House of Lords go back to the early Middle Ages, when they, along with abbots, represented some of the powerful landed interests in the country and were among the Monarch's chief advisers. Until the Reformation the Lords Spiritual usually outnumbered the lay members of the House of Lords. They remained a significant minority of the House of Lords until the mid-nineteenth century, when their number was capped at 26 and the number of new lay peerages soared. This trend continued and was reinforced by the introduction of life peerages in 1958.[6]

As we shall see, the role that bishops play in the House of Lords very much depends on the role that bishops play in the Church of England at large, which is itself the product of continuing evolution and change. Medhurst and Moyser chart the development of the episcopal role within the Church of England over the last three hundred years, describing three main eras. The eighteenth and early nineteenth century was the era of the "Prince bishop" during which bishops:

> [E]xercised something akin to absolute monarchial authority which owed more to social assumptions, nurtured in feudal society, than to theological insight. They were regarded as integral parts of one relatively cohesive governing class; though not always drawn from aristocratic families, they certainly came to be closely associated with the landed aristocracy and therefore tended to be seen as remote from the generality of parsons and parishioners.[7]

The era of the bishop as "Prelate" traversed the late nineteenth and much of the twentieth century. During this time, in the context of an industrialized society, "clerics tended to be driven back in the direction of their core ecclesiastical functions and so became more socially marginal figures."[8] The third era, from the 1960s to the present, sees the bishop primarily as "the Pastor."[9] Medhurst and Moyser describe this development as being a movement from the bishop "being an omni-competent decision-maker to the bishop thinking of himself as 'the animator', 'the enabler', 'the supporter', or 'encourager' within his diocese."[10] In practice, this development means that "for most contemporary bishops, pastoral activity in the diocese rates rather higher than national involvement" (be that in the central organs of the Church or within Parliament).[11] The establishment of the Crown Appointments' Commission in 1977 played a crucial role in creating this shift to a diocesan focus by giving, as it did, the diocese far greater involvement in the selection of its bishop. Owen Chadwick describes the input of diocesan representatives in the selection of their bishop:

> Normally the diocese asked for someone who was a good pastor and physically fit and therefore not too old. Quite often they would ask for someone of an ecumenical spirit who would not disturb the good relations between the denominations in that diocese ... [Q]uite often they would ask for someone who would not be too involved in outside commitments. They wanted a diocesan pastor rather than a national figure.[12]

If most bishops now devote very little time to exerting social and political influence, we could put this down to four factors.[13] Firstly, the theological understanding of the role of bishops has been revised. A bishop is now seen as "pastor and servant rather than prince and hierarchical superior", causing the bishops to focus upon facilitating the Christian service of his congregation within the political realm, not on acting as "the Church's chief or sole authoritative spokesman." Secondly, there are theological and cultural "constraints pointing clerical leaders towards a quest for consensus and harmony rather than confrontation and conflict". Thirdly, there are constraints placed upon bishops by the changing demands of their office. Amongst other things, the introduction of Synodical government has increased the bishops' workload and decreased the authority with which they can lead the Church's contribution to public debate. Fourthly, bishops are without the appropriate resources, particularly at the local level, needed for them to "discharge their task with suitably high levels of information or expertise". However, the selfsame process of episcopal disengagement from the society's ruling hierarchies has also given rise to:

> *This shift in emphasis, along with a wider disengagement of Church and State and the alleged - if ultimately fallacious - secularization of Britain in the late twentieth century, has made bishops outsiders in political debate.*

[A]n episcopal bench to some degree more at odds with traditional social and political arrangements and more disposed to take critical or even radical political stands or to be favourably disposed towards those in their immediate pastoral care who might do so. This is not to say that the overall level of political involvement of the Church has necessarily increased much as a result. But it is to say that the style and content of episcopal political contributions is shifting in ways which certainly give the impression, through their historical novelty, of a greater degree of political concern and activism.[14]

This shift in emphasis, along with a wider disengagement of Church and State and the alleged - if ultimately fallacious - secularization of Britain in the late twentieth century, has made bishops outsiders in political debate, and their Christian world-view rarely has any part in the formulation of the policies they have come to debate and vote upon. In theory, it stands to reason that they will, therefore, be eager to make full use of the opportunities and to exert their influence and the Christian perspective they represent.[15] Yet for many years, the criticism has been that the Church of England has failed to take full advantage of the opportunities that its presence in the House of Lords affords.

Church and State

Having said that the presence of the bishops in the House of Lords is not an element of establishment, it is nonetheless important to acknowledge that establishment has been the context in which bishops have worked out their involvement in our political institutions for more than four hundred years. Yet establishment is difficult to describe, taking many different forms over time.[16] Latterly, the 1970 Chadwick Commission simply defined it as simply "the laws which apply to the Church of England and not to other churches".[17]

The Church of England's special relationship with the State carries with it attendant "rights and privileges" and accompanying "restrictions and limitations".[18] In other words, the benefits that have accrued to the Church of England by virtue of establishment have come, and continue to come, at a price - namely, the intrusion of political authority into matters that in other churches would be the preserve of internal authorities:

> The established nature of the Church of England requires ... that some, if no longer all, decisions of the General Synod are themselves subject to approval (or very occasionally disapproval) by Parliament. And how is it possible to justify the continuation of this system when Parliament itself is made up of an enormous variety of individuals, of different faiths and none, most of whom have no interest in the internal affairs of the Church of England? The answer can only be a pragmatic one: that the system - curious though it may be - rarely causes a major problem, though the unexpected check to Synodical policy can and does occur. On a more theoretical level the argument becomes more difficult.[19]

Today, as a result of a series of modifications to the Church-State relationship since the 1960s, the Church has greater freedom than it did in the first half of the century.[20] For example, in the context of the appointment of bishops, Bernard Palmer observes that "the sting has largely been removed with the setting up of the Crown Appointments' Commission", (there have been one or two recent and notable exceptions). Julian Rivers goes further than Palmer, arguing that the restraints imposed upon the Church by establishment are now so minimal that there is little that a "spiritually vigorous" Church of England could not achieve.[21]

The relaxation of ties binding Church to State has opened up space within which the Church is essentially free to articulate a distinctive view of political matters. That the Church of England is the spiritual apologist for the actions of the government is an accusation rarely levelled of late, and on a host of issues the Church of England has challenged administrations of both colours. And whilst the Church's established status has the potential to hinder it in whatever political objectives it seeks to pursue, it nonetheless affords a number and variety of opportunities which other Christian denominations and other religions (and non-religions) do not benefit from.

David Rogers, reflecting on the benefits of establishment to the Church of England's role as a campaigning organization points out that:

> It has the things which other charities and lobbying groups value and work to obtain: a brand name which is instinctively recognised; royal patronage; access to opinion-formers, decision-makers and government; a professional staff at Church House and Lambeth Palace, many of whom come from the ranks of the civil service, who understand the business of government; a network of local organizations and an army of volunteers willing to do the drudgery work. Thanks to the fact that it is an established church, it has a leader, the Archbishop of Canterbury, who can be effective on the world stage, in a way that is out of proportion to the actual numbers in the Church.[22]

This begs the question, is establishment any longer appropriate or beneficial in a plural society, either for the Church of England or the UK's other faith communities? According to Richard Harries (formerly Bishop of Oxford), there is little support for disestablishment amongst the UK's non-Christian faith communities (those who appear to be most disadvantaged under existing arrangements).[23] Grace Davie quotes Adrian Hastings (a Roman Catholic),[24] Tariq Modood (a Muslim), and Jonathan Sacks (the Chief Rabbi)[25] to make the same point as Harries. The perspective offered by Modood is outlined in an article published in the *British Political Quarterly*. He writes:

> *For all who maintain a religious world-view in what to many people feels like an increasingly secular context, the established status of the Church of England acts as an institutional assurance that faith perspectives will receive some recognition.*

> I have to state as a brute fact that I have not come across a single article or speech or statement by any minority faith in favour of disestablishment. This is quite extraordinary given that secular reformers make the desire to accommodate these minorities an important motive for reform.[26]

For all who maintain a religious world-view in what to many people feels like an increasingly secular context, the established status of the Church of England acts as an institutional assurance that faith perspectives will receive some recognition. If and when religious representation in the second chamber broadens, this assurance will surely become less significant. Until then, the notion of a single ecumenical and interfaith community - a kind of collective of faiths which the Church of England can be seen to represent, albeit in an extremely vague way - will remain part of the episcopal approach to the House of Lords:

> The bishops are here not primarily to speak for the Church of England, narrowly conceived as a denomination, but for the spiritual and moral needs of the whole community. That is why we have stood for holding on to the best of our inheritance as we seek a more representative and inclusive shape to the whole House, including its spiritual aspects.[27]

a parting of ways

> The love that asks no questions, the love that stands the test, that lays upon the altar the dearest and the best.
>
> "I Vow To Thee, My Country"

If the establishment of the Church of England has meant a strong identification of the interests of the Church with those of the State, there is mounting evidence that the leadership of the Church of England increasingly feels that this is a deeply inappropriate position for the Christian community to occupy. Commenting on the words of the hymn, "I Vow to thee, My Country", Steven Lowe, Bishop of Hulme, said:

> It actually says we're going to support my country whatever it says, entire and whole and perfect, the love unquestioned, which is in the first verse of the hymn, right or wrong. That, I'm afraid, is actually heretical because it actually says that my country's approach to things must be my first call on myself and that my relationship with God or what I believe to be right or wrong is secondary to that ... I don't think anybody could actually say they could adopt an approach whereby they said they would not ask any questions of their government and their policies and so on.[28]

His comments reflect the development of an increasingly defiant mood in the Church of England, which can be traced back to both the loosening of constitutional ties and the changing political landscape in Britain over the last 30 years. This began in earnest with the Thatcher administration, under which the Church-State came to be characterized by tension and polarization. Over economic policy, unemployment, education, foreign policy and defence, immigration and race relations, and over the *Faith in the City* report, Church and State, working from contrasting philosophical foundations, came into conflict. From one point of view, it can be persuasively argued that the Church of England provided much-needed constructive political opposition during the 1980s.[29] In his biography David Sheppard, late Bishop of Liverpool, reserved fierce criticism for the Thatcherite economic agenda:

> Seeing life "from below" made me feel keenly the effects of some Government policies. The 1980 Budget made me feel ashamed to be British. It cut taxes for those who were best off and maintained allowances, mainly benefiting those without children to support. At the same time, it reduced the value of most of the benefits of working families.[30]

The Thatcher and Blair administrations are often paralleled. In both cases large parliamentary majorities have resulted in weakened oppositions, and have been built around reforming domestic agendas, relying on a novel philosophical approach (new right v. third way). Like Thatcher's, Blair's premiership has been marked out by controversial foreign policy and military conflicts, and has managed the mixing of a socially liberal approach on some issues with a striking authoritarianism in others. If in 1997 anyone hoped for a period of time when the voice of the Church and of the bishops in the House of Lords might have rubbed with the green a little more, the New Labour administration will have been a disappointment. Even on Labour issues like urban deprivation, the Church remains critical. In his introduction to *Faithful Cities*, the follow-up report to *Faith in the City*, the Archbishop of Canterbury conceded that the questions of 2006 were "as sharp" as those in 1985. The report argues:

> While Government policies have reduced poverty and stimulated economic growth, in other respects, the picture is less promising. Marked poverty and inequality persist, despite record levels of employment and nearly a decade of consistent economic growth... however prosperous a country, if there is a yawning gap between rich and poor, there is a corrosive effect on society. Income poverty has increased during the 1980s and 1990s: from 13% in 1979, to 25% in 1996-97 and 21% in 2003-04.[31]

There are, of course, changes as well as continuities. Certainly, the Labour Government has sought to enlist faith communities in tackling deprivation, and has pursued a line on international development which has been popular in the churches at large. Nevertheless, such conflicts continue to give the impression that the Church of England has somehow become more and more left-wing politically. In reality the Church's political instincts have probably remained in essentially the same place as they were in 1945. Rather, the Church's voice sounded radical and appeared increasingly left-wing because the political context into which it spoke had changed.

> *In reality the Church's political instincts have probably remained in essentially the same place as they were in 1945.*

a House for the future

As we look towards the future of religious representation and further reform of the House of Lords, it is worth rehearsing the basic constitutional facts. The incumbents of the dioceses of Canterbury, York, London, Durham and Winchester sit by right in the Lords (so holding the only *ex officio* seats in the Lords). The remaining twenty-one places are filled on the basis of seniority, measured from the date of first appointment to a diocesan See.[32] The Bishop of Sodor and Man (who sits in the House of Keys) and the Bishop of Gibraltar are ineligible to sit in the Lords. When a bishop retires he loses his seat, though some with significant public standing are afterwards given life peerages, notable examples of which include David Sheppard after his retirement as Bishop of Liverpool and Richard Harries, formerly Bishop of Oxford. Statutory retirement at the age of 70 means that the length of any individual's involvement in the House is often short, particularly in the context of the lifelong membership of all other members of the House. Currently, only the Bishops of London, Southwark and Winchester have sat in the House for over ten years.

The current ongoing process of constitutional reform was heralded by the Labour Party's 1997 manifesto commitment to "carry out a careful and considered reform of the House of Lords: the immediate removal of the hereditary peerage, and longer-term reform of the House of Lords as a whole".

The initial result of this "radical and historic task" was the publication of a White Paper (January 1999) in which, most significantly, the Labour Government committed itself to legislating to remove the rights of hereditary peers to sit and vote in the House of Lords and to appoint a Royal Commission to make recommendations for a wide-ranging reform of the second chamber.[33] The rights of all but 92 hereditary peers to sit and vote in the House were duly removed in November 1999 and a Royal Commission, chaired by Lord Wakeham, with broad terms of reference to consider the role, functions and composition of the second chamber met from March to December 1999, publishing its report, *A House for the Future*, in January 2000.

A House for the Future contained 132 recommendations, 9 of which related to the representation of religious faiths, the most significant of which include:

> The Church of England should continue to be explicitly represented in the second chamber, but the concept of religious representation should be broadened to embrace other Christian denominations, in all parts of the United Kingdom, and other faith communities. (Recommendation 108).

> The Appointments' Commission should ensure that at any one time there are at least five members of the second chamber specifically selected to be broadly representative of the different non-Christian faith communities. (Recommendation 109).[34]

> The total number of places in the reformed second chamber for members formally representing the various Christian denominations throughout the United Kingdom should be 26. Taking into account the relative size of the population in each of the nations which comprise the United Kingdom, 21 of these places should go to members representing the Christian denominations in England and 5 should go to members representing the Christian denominations in Scotland, Wales and Northern Ireland. (Recommendation 110).

> Of the 21 places available for members of the Christian denominations in England, 16 should be assigned to representatives of the Church of England and 5 to members of other Christian denominations in England. (Recommendation 111).

The Church of England should review the options for providing formal Church of England representation in the reformed second chamber. Their detailed recommendations should be made to the Government in time for incorporation into whatever legislation is required to implement our own recommendations. (Recommendation 115).

Regarding the broadening of religious representation in the Lords, the Commission observed that there are a range of obstacles which would need to be overcome. These include the fact that virtually all faiths (and many other Christian denominations) other than the Anglican Church lack the kind of structure that could easily deliver appointees to the second chamber. Even those that do (for example, the Roman Catholic Church or the Church of Scotland) may have practical or theological concerns with taking up seats in the Lords. Ultimately, the Wakeham Commission's *modus operandi* would involve consulting relevant ecumenical bodies for Christian denominations, and reserving five places which the Appointments' Commission would look to fill with representatives of other faiths, in consultation with interfaith organizations and such representative bodies that exist.

The House of Lords: Completing the Reform, a second Government White Paper published in November 2001, sets out "...how the Government intends to deliver its 2001 Manifesto pledge to implement the Royal Commission report in the most effective way possible."[35] It states that: "The Government acknowledges the force of the Royal Commission's proposition that religious representation helps in the recognition of the part that moral, philosophical and theological considerations have to play in debating political and social issues." Likewise, the White Paper accepts the Royal Commission's proposal that there should be a formal representation for the Church of England and that this representation should be reduced numerically, from 26 to 16 places.[36]

The Government's invitation for responses to all the proposals contained in *The House of Lords: Completing the Reform* was accepted by the Archbishops' Council whose unpublished response was sent to the Lord Chancellor and the Prime Minister on 31 January 2002. As expected, the Church's response did not greet warmly either the proposal to reduce the Church of England's representation to 16 or the failure to provide for formal representation for other denominations and faiths:

> Our belief remains that a total presence of twenty bishops is the minimum necessary to maintain the parliamentary service we seek to offer. We also continue to believe that there should be a defined overall number of places for other Christian churches and other faiths.[37]

In February 2002, the Public Administration Select Committee published *The Second Chamber: Continuing the Reform*,[38] recommending that the size of the House be cut, with 60% of its membership elected, 20% appointed by party, and 20% appointed independents. As a consequence of the overall reduction in size, and on the understanding that the presence of the bishops is a "mediaeval hangover", the report called for the removal of bishops as members of the second chamber (though the Appointments' Commission would be free to appoint bishops if they so chose).

Since this point, there has been little real progress. The debate, orbiting chiefly around the question of composition by appointment and election, came to a head when Lord Lloyd of Berwick moved an amendment at the Second Reading of the Constitutional Reform Bill on 8 March 2004, committing the Bill to a Select Committee. The amendment was carried by 216 votes to 183, and prompted the Government to shelve its proposals, arguing that the vote made it "abundantly clear" that the House of Lords would not pass the Bill and committing to revisit the issue in upcoming manifestos. Cynics felt, with some justification, that reform was dead in the water. However, responding to a Westminster Hall debate on 20 June 2006' Nigel Griffiths, Deputy Leader of the House of Commons, confirmed that the Leader of the House, Jack Straw, had been given responsibility for continuing the process of reform, and that he was already pursuing informal meetings:

> *...the management of a public space that includes a plurality of religious and non-religious convictions is clearly one of the most pressing political problems of the twenty-first century.*

The Government have made it clear that they would prefer to proceed with Lords reform by consensus ... One of the frustrating things about Lords reform is that there is a large degree of agreement about the fundamentals, yet we cannot find a clear way forward.[39]

The role of religious representation in a reformed House is not an issue that is, or should be, counted among "the fundamentals". Nonetheless, it is one that should be pursued with vigour: the management of a public space that includes a plurality of religious and non-religious convictions is clearly one of the most pressing political problems of the twenty-first century. In view of a shifting political landscape, establishment has long since ceased to be the paradigm through which the relationship of the State and the Church of England can be easily understood, let alone the relationship between the State and minority faiths. Religious representation in the House of Lords could be one element of a new and more open settlement between the religious communities and the nation at large.

In principle, what role should faith have in our national political institutions? There are, of course, those who dream of a utopia of secularized political institutions from which the remaining vestiges of religious interference are removed. They ignore the fact that every historical attempt to create a secular political space has failed. Indeed, there is no logical connection between a secular constitution and a secular political environment - the United States is one example, Turkey another. Even here, the growing role of religion in civil society means that attempts to secularize political institutions are unlikely to succeed.

More than this, religious leaders have a different kind of relationship with communities than those that are defined by democratic election. These relationships are often built on a strong sense of practical responsibility, a shared world-view, and love. The Church of England, for example, maintains a continuous physical presence in communities where Government ministers would fear to occasionally tread. Indeed, some of the bishops that eventually take up a seat in the House of Lords will have spent time serving in and coming to know the breadth of needs that those communities have.

Nevertheless, the role of the bishops in the Lords has been viewed with some asperity by both members of the House of Lords, and by critics from within the Church of England. It is widely thought, in the light of their not insignificant numbers, that they fail to take advantage of the opportunity that their seats provide and that their impact is "benign but not dramatic".[40] Proposals for the future of religious representation in a reformed House must be considered in the light not only of issues of principle, but also in view of how religious representation is working in practice.

introduction - references

1. David Starkey, "Henry was wrong. Put religion back in its box", The *Sunday Times*, 12 November 2006 David Starkey's comparison is a false one - the Assembly of Experts and Council of Guardians are part of the executive branch of Iran's Government, not its legislature.
2. F Bown, "Influencing the House of Lords: the Role of the Lords Spiritual 1979-1987", *Political Studies*, XLII (1994), p. 105
3. H Montefiore in an interview with the author, 21 May 2002
4. Royal Commission on the Reform of the House of Lords, *A House for the Future*, Command Paper 4534, p. 152 (15.8). See also Avis, *Church, State and Establishment*, p. 21
5. Michael L Nash, "The Leaven in the Lump: Bishops in the House of Lords." *Contemporary Review*, 1999
6. Royal Commission on the Reform of the House of Lords, *A House for the Future*, Command Paper 4534, p.150 (15.1)
7. KN Medhurst & GH Moyser, *Church and Politics in a Secular Age*, p. 78
8. *ibid.*, p. 79
9. *ibid.*, pp. 78-82
10. *ibid.*, p. 113. John Whale presents a similar analysis, emphasising the modern managerial aspects of a bishop's role: "Besides being representatives, they are managers, particularly of their clergy." See J Whale, *The Anglican Church Today*, p. 43. See also T Beeson, *The Bishops*, p. 1
11. KN Medhurst & GH Moyser, "Lambeth Palace, the Bishops and Politics", GH Moyser (ed.), *Church and Politics Today*, p. 77
12. O Chadwick, *Michael Ramsey*, pp. 129-130.
13. KN Medhurst & GH Moyser, "Lambeth Palace, the Bishops and Politics", GH Moyser (ed.), *Church and Politics Today*, pp. 79-82
14. GH Moyser, "The Church of England and Politics: Patterns and Trends", GH Moyser (ed.), *Church and Politics Today*, p. 20
15. Jeff Haynes makes a related point in relation to trends throughout Western Europe: "The concern of institutional religious elites to make public pronouncements on social and politics issues is a growing feature in much of Western Europe. It is, in effect, an attempt to deprivatize religion from where the process of secularization seems to be sending it: to socio-political marginality." J Haynes, *Religion in Global Politics*, p. 68
16. P Avis, *Church, State and Establishment*, p. 21
17. Archbishop of Canterbury's Commission on Church and State, *Church and State*, The Chadwick Report, p. 2
18. PA Welsby, *How the Church of England Works*, p. 45. See also P Avis, *Church, State and Establishment*, p. 36
19. G Davie, *Religion in Modern Britain*, p. 144
20. B Palmer, *High and Mitred*, pp. 1-2. See also Furlong, *Church of England*, pp. 236-237
21. J Rivers, "Disestablishment and the Church of England", Schluter (ed.), *Christianity in a Changing World*, p. 79
22. D Rogers, *Politics, Prayer and Parliament*, p. 142
23. R Harries, Why we need faith in the Lords, *Church Times*, 24 May 2002
24. A Hastings, *Church and State: The English Experience* (Exeter University Press, 1991), pp. 75-76
25. J Sacks, *The Persistence of Faith* (London: Weidenfeld, 1991), p. 68
26. T Modood, "Ethno-religious minorities, Secularism and the British State", *British Political Quarterly* (1994), pp. 61-65

27 The Bishop of Guildford, Lords Hansard, 4 July 2002, col. 357
28 http://www.bbc.co.uk/radio4/today/reports/arts/vow_20040813.shtml
29 G Davie, *Religion in Modern Britain*, p. 39
30 David Sheppard, *Steps Along Hope Street*, p. 193
31 *Faithful Cities*, Archbishop's Council 2006
32 D Shell, *The House of Lords*, p. 30
33 Government White Paper, *Modernising Parliament: Reforming the House of Lords*, Command Paper 4183, p. iii
34 In the context of Recommendation 115 the Wakeham report expresses concern that "unless the number of eligible bishoprics were reduced, or the basis of Church of England representation altered, bishops would in future need to wait up to ten years before becoming members of the second chamber and could then only expect to serve for three or four years". It also indicates a preference for Church of England representatives who would be able to serve a 15-year term in the House of Lords. It leaves the resolution of these issues to the Church of England.
35 Government White Paper, *The House of Lords: Completing the Reform*, p. 4
36 *ibid.* p. 29
37 Archbishops' Council, *Comments from the Church of England on the Government's White Paper* (Unpublished: January 2002)
38 House of Commons Paper 494, session 2001-02
39 House of Commons Hansard, 20 June 2006, col. 384WH
40 Christopher Morgan, *Playing a part in the Lords*, Church of England Newspaper.

1

do bishops attend?

The Church of England's submission to the Wakeham Commission on the Reform of the House of Lords claims that "[b]ishops maintain a constant attendance in the second chamber so that the Church is always in a position to respond to the issues of the day."[41] Certainly, the staff at Lambeth Palace arrange for a duty bishop to be assigned for every day that the House is sitting. His duty is to lead prayers in the Upper House at the beginning of the day's business.[42] A list is circulated amongst the bishops (the most senior bishops receive it first, although the Bishoprics of Canterbury, York, London, Durham and Winchester are exempted from the system) for them to sign up for two or three weeks at the House during which, according to one former bishop they are "supposed to be there all day for any business right up to closing time at ten o'clock or whenever it is..."[43] The use of the word "supposed" suggests that the constant attendance claimed by the Church (a claim heavily dependent on the notion of the duty bishops) reflects the intention more than the execution. Commenting on the attendance of the Lords Spiritual more generally, Donald Shell proposes that:

> Bishops are busy people, and attendance at the House of Lords has to be fitted in around a very full schedule... Some bishops give much more attention to the Lords than others, but very few in recent years have attended more than one-third of the sitting-days.[44]

Commentators have argued that, in view of the sheer variety in the attendance records of the bishops (even taking into account the varying length of their periods of eligibility to attend), episcopal attendance is essentially dependent upon the individual personality, experience, expertise and priorities of each bishop.[45] For example, in the 2004-05 session (unusually short because of the General Election), the Bishop of Sheffield made no appearances at all, while the Bishop of Southwark and the Bishop of Oxford made 40 (over 60% of sitting days) and 27 (just under 50% of sitting days) appearances respectively, consistent with their reputation as two of the most active prelates in the Lords *(see fig. 1.1)*.

This assessment fits with the submission which the bishops made to the Jellicoe Committee on the workings of the House of Lords during 1971, which indicates that a minority of diocesans were simply not keen to be involved in the business of the House of Lords. It also reveals that, for those bishops (the majority) who did see it as a valuable opportunity, it always came below the diocese on their list of priorities.[46] Certainly, bishops as a group have a poor attendance rate. In 1996-97, the last session under Conservative administration, only 11% of Lords Spiritual attended more than one third of sittings compared with 56% of life peers, and no single bishop attended more that two thirds of sittings in the session.

fig. 1.1

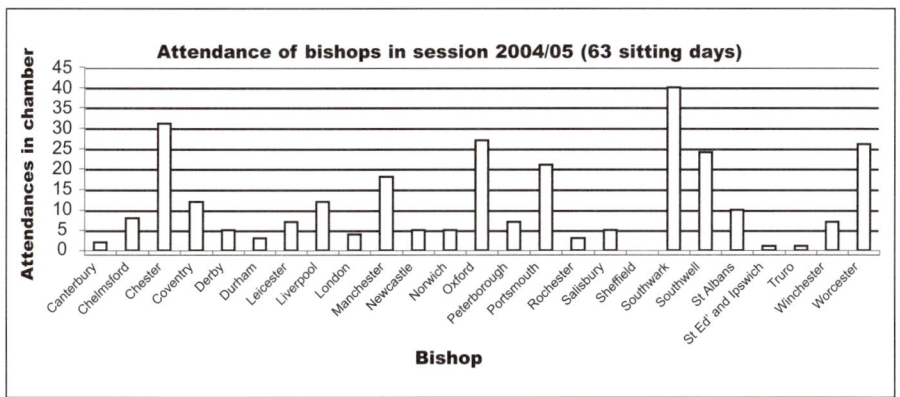

When we look at the statistical picture over time we see that, alongside the continuing variety between bishops, there is a clear upward trend in episcopal attendance. Research carried out by Francis Bown into the contribution of the bishops to the House of Lords during the period of May 1979 to May 1987 shows the average bishop as being in attendance at the House on just 12% of sitting days.[47] In contrast, figures for the sessions 1997-98 to 2004-05 indicate a steadily rising attendance rate, moving above the 18% mark in the session 2004-05, which represents around 5 to 8 more attendances per bishop, per session *(fig. 1.2)*.

It may be reasonable to complain that bishops don't attend much, but they are attending more than they used to.

fig.1.2

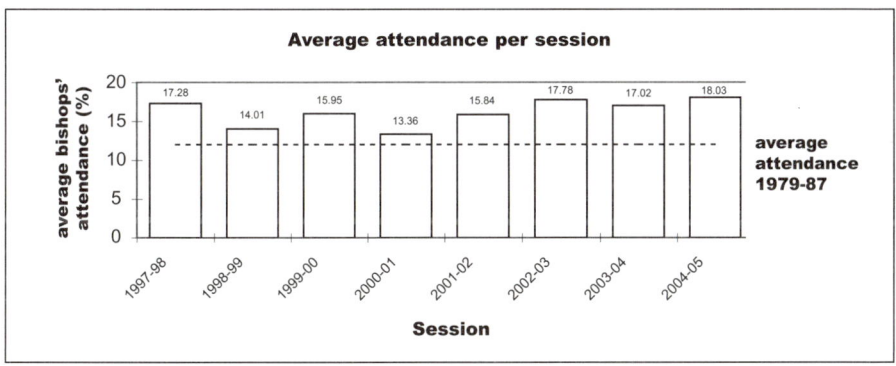

Equally, the number of bishops attending on each sitting day is increasing against figures in the 1980s *(fig.1.3)*. It may be reasonable to complain that bishops don't attend much, but they are attending more than they used to.

fig. 1.3

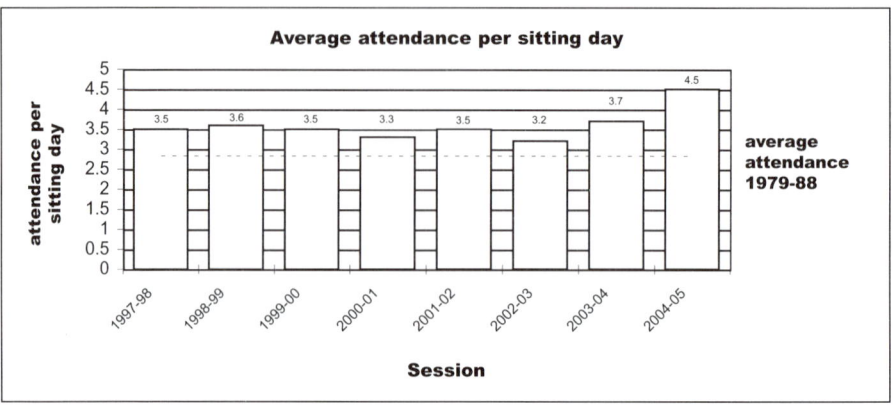

how significant is increased attendance?

Whether one is critical or sympathetic in principle to the notion of religious representation in the Lords, it is important to note that, for religious leaders, their effectiveness could never be measured by attendance alone. Remarkably, the controversial figure of David Jenkins (Bishop of Durham), who was one of the most publicly recognizable bishops during the 1980s, visited the House of Lords on only 13 occasions. He gives the following explanation for his limited attendance at the House:

> Attendance in the Lords always involved me, if I were to speak, in two days away from the diocese. The notice would also be pretty short-term, so my London visit was bound to clash with some pre-existing engagement locally. This meant that I had to balance the priority between my commitments locally and the likelihood of my appearance in the Lords making any difference there or elsewhere.[48]

The effect of geographical proximity to the Palace of Westminster is, in fact, not immediately clear. Although this will undoubtedly make it easier for bishops who are minded to take a greater part in the business of the House, it is also the case that the Bishop of London only managed four appearances in the 2004/05 session, while the Bishop of Chester came to the House on 31 occasions, albeit some as duty bishop, and often made substantive contributions.

While indicating some increased commitment to a national and public role, these statistics give succour to those who would call for a review of the internal structures that determine which bishops sit. On the basis of attendance alone, we can already argue that the key driver for greater involvement is individual personality, experience, expertise and priorities, yet, considering there are only 42 eligible diocesan bishops at any one time, an individual of whatever character or disposition will probably end up in the Lords if he happens not to die or retire. There is, then, a strong case for considering a system which would ensure a decisive shift away from the present determinative - that of seniority - to a process of selection which takes into account the disposition of the individual. A change of this type would ensure that those increasingly valuable places would be occupied by individual bishops committed, and able, to make use of the opportunity to contribute to the House. Equally, it would help to ensure that bishops who are ill-equipped (for whatever reason) to contribute to parliamentary life are not required to expend their energies away from their calling within the diocese and the national structures of the Church. The reform resulting from such a review would necessarily involve a weakening of the link between the bishop and his diocese - whether to a greater extent (through the formation of specialist "political bishops" who are free from diocesan responsibilities) or to a lesser extent (through growing dependence on suffragan bishops ministering to the diocese).

Again, however, arguments cannot be built on frequency of attendance alone (attendance in the chamber might indicate commitment, but not necessarily efficacy). Moreover, attendance of members of the House of Lords as a whole has not been a criterion for reform. The fact that peers are not, for the most part, professional politicians is usually seen as a strong advantage of the existing system - Lords Spiritual and Temporal are able to benefit from a wider understanding and professional experience. As we consider broader religious representation, it is worth asking the question of how often a religious representative in the Lords would be expected to attend to justify their place.

chapter 1 - references

41 Archbishops' Council, *The Role of the Bishops in the Second Chamber*, p. 8
42 A Hastings, *Robert Runcie*, p. 85
43 JB Taylor in an interview with the author, 29 July 2002
44 D Shell, *The House of Lords*, pp. 54-55
45 KN Medhurst & GH Moyser, "Lambeth Palace, the Bishops and Politics", Moyser (ed.), *Church and Politics Today*, p. 77
46 O Chadwick, *Michael Ramsey*, p. 183
47 F Bown, "Influencing the House of Lords: the Role of the Lords Spiritual, 1979-1987", *Political Studies*, XLII (1994), p. 107
48 D Jenkins in a letter to the author, 13 May 2002

do bishops vote?

"It is well understood," argues Lord Longford, "that it is almost impossible for bishops to preserve a high record of voting. They remain a minor factor in the politics of the House."[49] The obvious retort for defenders of the episcopal contribution is that it is hardly the role of the bishops to seek to influence the outcome of any and every vote in the House of Lords but, whichever way you look at it, rates of voting amongst the bishops are lower than amongst other groups of peers.

Francis Bown's research indicates a limited role for the bishops: between 1979 and 1987, the bishops took part in only 21.4% of the divisions of the House of Lords.[50] Bown's research also reveals that it was exceedingly rare for more than two bishops to vote in the same division, asserting that only 3.9% of the divisions of the House involved more than two bishops.[51] Contemporary data also supports the view that rates of voting amongst bishops have generally been low. Indeed over the course of the whole of Margaret Thatcher's premiership, the bishops voted in a slightly greater proportion (22.9%) of the divisions of the House than records for the period from 1979-87 (21.4%). Again, later research supports the assertion that it was rare for the division lobbies to receive more than one bishop during a single division, presenting two or more bishops as having voted in 7.1% of the total divisions of the House over the course of the whole of the 1980s.

> ...it is hardly the role of the bishops to seek to influence the outcome of any and every vote in the House of Lords but, whichever way you look at it, rates of voting amongst the bishops are lower than amongst other groups of peers.

Again, however, it seems that there has been a marked rise in the frequency of episcopal voting in recent sessions. There were 641 divisions of the House in the 2001-05 Parliament, with a bishop participating in 298 (see *fig. 2.1*).

fig. 2.1

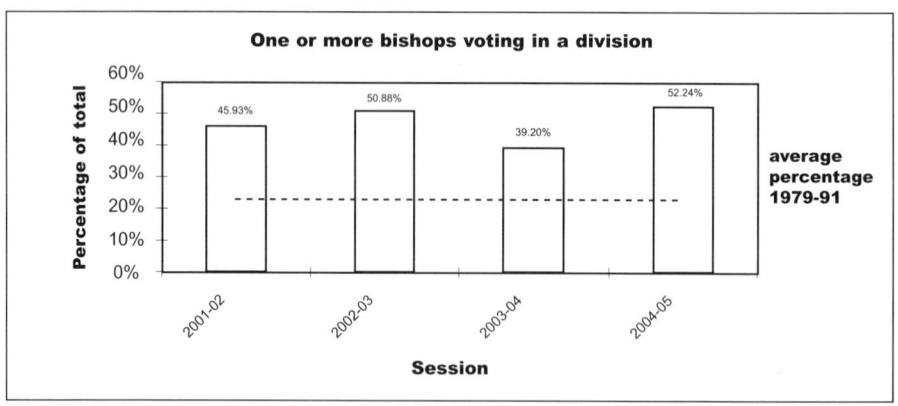

Remarkably, our research also shows that in this Parliament two or more bishops voted in 21.5% of divisions, and three or more in 10.85% divisions. Put simply, there has been a tripling in the frequency of multiple (more than two) bishops voting in the same division (see fig. 2.2). So, while attendance has risen modestly, it seems that when a prelate does attend he is considerably more likely to vote. It is initially difficult to account for the rise in voting. One hypothesis could be that there are considerably more close votes (and so votes where an individual may feel that voting might be significant) than there were under previous administrations. We address this at greater length below.

fig. 2.2

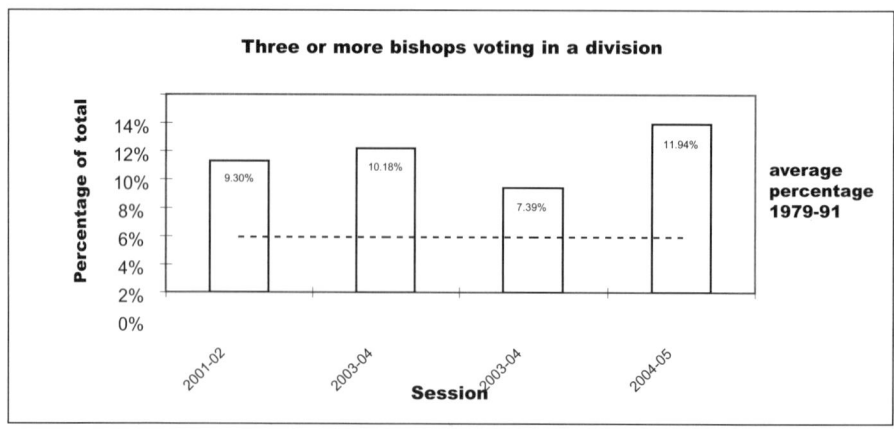

opposing the government of the day

When the bishops are voting, Shell points out that they:

> [D]o not appear to show any inhibition in voting against the Government, or even helping to bring about a Government defeat ... In the 1980s tensions between the Church of England and Mrs Thatcher's Conservative Government became very obvious, and the bishops in the Lords found themselves voting against the Government much more frequently than in its support.[52]

Under the Thatcher administration, statistics present a ratio of 2:1 between anti-government and pro-government votes. The bishops were also ten times as likely to vote in a division which resulted in a government defeat. In spite of this, it would be in no way concurrent with the data on the bishops' voting record during the Thatcher years to argue that they sought to use their voting rights in an aggressive or united manner in an effort to alter the outcome of divisions. In just 4% of the total number of divisions in which the bishops voted did six or more of them vote together, providing the level of numerical strength with the potential to alter the outcome of a division. This is not to say that on occasions the bishops did not vote in a manner which makes it clear that they did intend to do their utmost to alter the outcome of the division, such as was the case with the divisions relating to the Shops' Bill (1986). The Bench of Bishops, therefore, has no qualms about voting against the Government.

Since 1997 the Labour Government has suffered a remarkably high number of defeats in the House of Lords (approaching 400 at the time of writing). We see again that bishops were participating at a higher rate in government defeats than in government victories. In the 1997-2001 Parliament there were 108 divisions resulting against the government whip, with one or more bishops voting 53 (49%) of these, two or more voting in 28 (25.9%), and three or more voting in 11 (10.2%). There is a marked discrepancy with the rate of episcopal voting in government victories. For instance, in the 1997-98 session, there were 140 divisions resulting in a government victory. One or more bishops voted in 46 (32.9%), two or more in 20 (14.3%), and three or more in only 3 (2.1%) divisions. Across the whole parliament, there were 380 government victories with bishops participating in 104 of these (36.8%), more than 2 in only 12 (3.2%). Bishops participate at even higher rates in unwhipped divisions (around 75% of unwhipped divisions saw one or more bishops through the lobbies). Again, however, it does not seem to be the case that bishops seek to, or are successful in, affecting the outcome of particular ballots. Meg Russell and Maria Sciara of the Constitution Unit, University College London, find the following:

> *...if the bishops are still not voting in sufficient numbers to change the outcome of individual divisions, do the bishops have an alternative collective understanding of what they are seeking to achieve with their votes?*

> [T]he votes of the bishops only rarely make a difference to legislative outcomes. Of our 806 divisions this occurred only four times. Once in 2004 on an amendment to the Pensions Bill where the government won by two votes, but without the support of two Bishops voting the result would have been a tie. On two occasions, in 2000 and 2003, the government was defeated by one vote, with the vote of one bishop making the difference between this and a tied vote. Only once, on the Nationality, Immigration and Asylum Bill in 2003, was the government defeated thanks to the votes of bishops, when otherwise it would have won.[53]

Again, we have a picture which sees the episcopal role as both limited, in the sense that they are voting at a relatively low rate, but growing in importance, in that they are voting more and in greater numbers. Yet if the bishops are still not voting in sufficient numbers to change the outcome of individual divisions, do the bishops have an alternative collective understanding of what they are seeking to achieve with their votes? Perhaps their approach can be summarized in the words of Michael Ramsey in a letter to Donald Coggan during March 1968. If in a reformed, more democratically credible, second chamber the bishops wish to retain their voting rights, they would do well to continue to vote in the same manner and to the same end, as Ramsey suggests:

> The episode [the passing of the Kenya Asians Bill in the House of Lords] sets me thinking again about the significance of voting in the House of Lords, and I feel that the purpose of our voting is to register opinions as a kind of witness and that if we become a body which tried to influence legislation by turning up in force we should be involved in all sorts of difficulties and our position would not be tolerated. I do, however, agree with those who have said in our recent discussion that if we are to maintain this kind of token voting there must be a good many of us from whom the votes can be forthcoming.[54]

chapter 2 - references

49 F Longford, *The Bishops*, p. 114
50 F Bown, "Influencing the House of Lords: the Role of the Lords Spiritual, 1979-1987", *Political Studies*, XLII (1994), p. 109
51 *ibid.*
52 D Shell, *The House of Lords*, p. 54
53 M Russell and M Sciara, *Why does the Government get defeated in the House of Lords?* - Paper to 2006 Political Studies Association Conference (5 April 2006). Available at http://www.ucl.ac.uk/constitution-unit
54 Letter from Michael Ramsey to Donald Coggan, 1 March 1968, cited by O Chadwick, *Michael Ramsey*, 184

3 do bishops speak?

> A bishop (occasionally more than one) will generally speak in a major public debate, including the second readings of Bills on questions of social policy ... It is however exceptional for the bishops to engage in sustained political pressure in the Lords for a particular purpose.[55]

This analysis of Giles Ecclestone, former Secretary of the Church of England Board for Social Responsibility, is shared by Medhurst and Moyser who comment that "[t]he contributions of most spiritual peers are spasmodic. In modern times few have been heavily involved in this arena". Perhaps the changing episcopal role and the added demands wrought by the introduction of Synodical government are the chief causes of this spasmodic speech-making.[56] In addition, we might add that the procedures of the House of Lords itself do not encourage episcopal contribution, where speakers in debates are expected to await official replies, and short official notice of forthcoming business does not allow enough time for bishops to plan their schedules so that they can incorporate preparation for, and attendance at, debates.[57]

However, Donald Shell does argue that few eligible bishops never contribute to a House of Lords' debate and that "in almost any area of legislation an episcopal contribution may be forthcoming."[58] The observation is a fair one: bishops can be heard speaking on subjects from telecommunications to airports to local government finance, and they have a particular penchant for a handful of specific issues, including heritage (the Church of England is responsible for over 80% of England's historic places of worship), education (through Church of England schools), and penal and health policy (through chaplaincies) and so on. Individual bishops often maintain a brief on a particular issue, and so are more likely to participate in such a debate. Increasingly, prelates are also initiating debates. Of course, there is a continuing preference for contributing to debates where a "moral dimension was self-evident."[59]

Equally, only 17 of the 51 individual bishops who did speak at the House of Lords during the Thatcher years made more than 10 contributions. In fact, these 17 individual bishops made 75% of the bishops' speeches to the House. Again, the variation in the level of contribution to the House made by each individual bishop, even taking into account the varying length of their periods of eligibility to attend the House, can only be accounted for in the same way as the variation in the attendance rate of the bishops - with reference to the individual personality, experience, expertise and priorities of each individual bishop.

However, in line with the growing politicization of the bishops, as expressed in increased attendance and voting, Lords Spiritual are taking a greater part in intervening in debate (see fig. 3.1). The high water mark of episcopal speech-making in the 1980s was the 1983/84 session, where the bishops as a whole made 105 contributions to the House of Lords' debates, way above the average number of contributions by session during the decade, which was 64. In stark contrast, in the 2005/06 session bishops spoke or intervened in around 130 separate debates.

Equally, while we have noted that only 17 of 51 bishops made more than 10 contributions under the Thatcher administration, of the bishops currently sitting in the House of Lords 4 have made more than 10 distinct contributions in this session alone. Only 8 of the 25 currently sitting have not made more than 10 contributions over the course of their parliamentary career. Currently, the most active speech-maker is the Bishop of Portsmouth who, over the course of an 8 year career, has personally contributed to nearly 170 separate debates. Although this is in part due to his role as Chair of the Church of England Board of Education (who is obliged to lead as often as possible on education issues in the light of the Church's role in the provision of education) he has easily surpassed the extent of speech-making under the most prolific bishops in the Thatcher years.

fig. 3.1

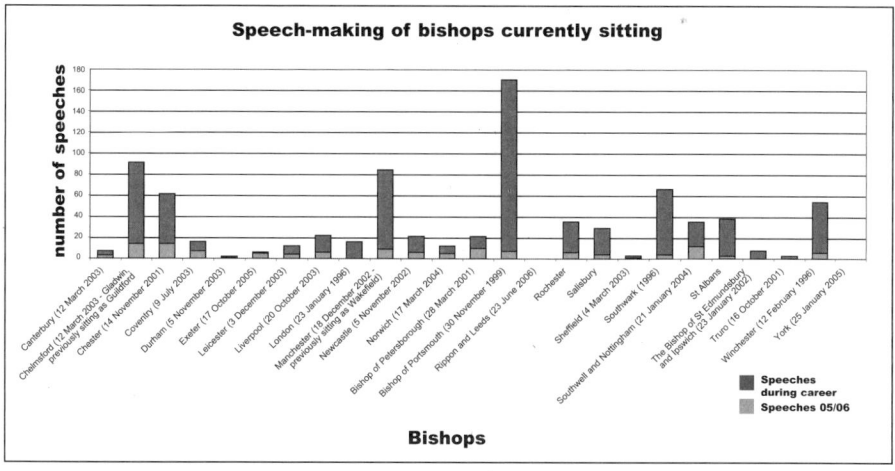

is the contribution significant?

> *It is important to note that participation is increasing both in reference to their record in previous years and in regard to Lords Temporal colleagues.*

The Church of England has been continually criticized by commentators for failing to take full advantage of the opportunities that their seats in the Lords provide. During the Thatcher years, the bishops spoke relatively little on matters on which the Church of England was widely known to be critical of the Government, specifically on Trade and Industry issues. Critics argue that the House of Lords clearly represents the most appropriate forum for the Church of England to enter into the national debate on any socio-political matter which should be the primary vehicle for it to vocalise its position in relation to government policies.

Detractors, particularly those within the Church of England, will still argue that the bishops do not contribute enough or on the right occasions. It is important to note, however, that participation is increasing both in reference to their record in previous years and in regard to Lords Temporal colleagues. The most trenchant critics might do well to reflect on this fact, as well as on the question of what benchmark bishops should be judged by, particularly given that their diocesan time commitments are, without exception, as demanding as that of a QC or senior business person. Comparison to working peers may not necessarily be appropriate.[60]

If the diary is still the greatest barrier to a bishop's participation, it is nonetheless unreasonable to expect that the procedures of the House will change in order to make attendance and speech-making for any minority group within its membership easier, for instance, by following the House of Commons and beginning sittings earlier in the day. As such, any strategy which the Church of England formulates to seek to increase the effectiveness of the bishops' contribution to the House of Lords would need to tackle this hindrance. First and foremost, such a strategy will need to set about creating a situation whereby those bishops who have been chosen to perform this aspect of the Church's public ministry have far greater flexibility to be at the House during the evenings and at short notice.

chapter 3 - references

55 G Ecclestone, *The Church of England and Politics*, pp. 50-51
56 KN Medhurst & GH Moyser, *Church and Politics in a Secular Age*, p. 274
57 *ibid.*
58 D Shell, *The House of Lords*, p. 54
59 *ibid.*, p. 55
60 For example, Baroness Helena Kennedy of Shaws, normally perceived as an effective legislator and social commentator, only spoke in ten debates in the 2005/06 session.

4

what do bishops say?

When bishops do speak the note they strike tends to be thoughtful rather than campaigning, faithful in fact to the character of most Lords debates, and reflecting an awareness that the Upper House can no longer claim an overriding say in major decisions of policy.[61]

Data indicates that an overwhelming proportion of bishops' speeches to the House do not take a definite position in relation to government policy, which supports Ecclestone's suggestion that episcopal contributions tend to be "...thoughtful rather than campaigning". This probably reflects the nature of the House of Lords, where the nature of debates means that contributions are often inquisitive, rather than accusative, in nature. There is some evidence to suggest that the episcopate in the Lords is becoming increasingly critical of government policy. An analysis of the speech-making of the Lords Spiritual during the Thatcher years paints the picture of an episcopate whose verbal contributions "...tended towards criticism of rather than support for the Conservative Government."[62] Equally, under Blair there are policy areas where the bishops consistently speak in a way which is implicitly or explicitly critical of government policy (one good example would be penal policy) and there have been notable pieces of legislation where individual bishops have taken issue and campaigned against a Bill, even in opposition to the views of their colleagues on the Bench of Bishops.

On most occasions where bishops contribute to the same debate their contributions are independent (bringing differing points to the issue under discussion). In terms of preparation, bishops do on occasion look to the staff of Church House for support and briefing, particularly when the issue is one of concern to the Anglican Church as a whole. Generally, however, they work under their own steam or even receive support and speech-writing from the political offices of other Christian denominations and various charities or interest groups. There are, of course, occasions when the bishops speak with a clearly united voice on a particular issue. Under the Thatcher administration, this would be particularly true of debates on apartheid and on Sunday trading. Under Blair, the clearest example is the recent debate on Churches and Cities, initated by the Archbishop of Canterbury, where a well-researched and pre-prepared party-line could be detected in each episcopal contribution. Equally, there are occasions, recently on the Civil Partnership Bill, where flatly contradictory messages are sent from the Bench of Bishops. This record fits with John B Taylor's description of how being present at the House of Lords as an individual Lord of Parliament, not a corporate spokesmen for the Anglican Church, affected the manner in which he approached his role:

You were aware that you had total freedom to say what you wanted to say. But essentially the things that you wanted to say would be representing the Church's view and you wanted to know what the Church's line was on a particular subject...[63]

A number of significant findings emerge from our analysis of the arguments used by the bishops to support the points that they made during their speeches in the House. The bishops' considerable use of experience-based arguments indicates how significant the link between the episcopal contributor and the diocese is in generating contributions which are authoritative in tone and distinctive in perspective. The bishops' considerable use of arguments based on facts, statistics, and academic and professional advice indicates a strong emphasis on influencing debates through the presentation of a well-informed and credible assessment of the issues under discussion. In this context it is also notable how limited, in relative terms, was the bishops' use of arguments which were evidently rooted in theological and moral considerations. Similarly, it is of note that biblical material was explicitly referred to in only 7% of episcopal contributions to the House during the 1980s. Just 1% of the bishops' speeches offered a thorough examination of biblical material. The bishops' implicit references to biblical teaching were more commonplace.

> *...it is also notable how limited, in relative terms, was the bishops' use of arguments which were evidently rooted in theological and moral considerations.*

There continues to be a surprising dearth of arguments that are rooted in theological or biblical perspectives, with bishops continuing to prefer contributions on diocesan experience, the views of experts, statistical analysis and so on. Occasionally, a speech is flavoured by an example from Church history, or a light reference to an ancient Christian thinker (the Bishop of Chester recently managed to relate Tertullian to a debate on football).[64] Of course, bishops, in part, are simply going about the business of building effective contributions, sensitive to the fact that the House may not respond well to reasoning or discourse rooted exclusively in Christian thinking - nevertheless, it does evidence a particular approach to public debate which does not leave much room for discourse rooted in any tradition other than the liberal:

> It should not need saying that treating religious groups as valid participants ... does not mean failing to scrutinise or criticise them. Indeed it means the very opposite. If religious groups wish to participate in this area of the public square, they must be willing to defend themselves without recourse to sectarian or inscrutable reasons. They must be self critical and willing to utilise (if also challenge) public reason. This is the price of admission.[65]

Recent debates on Assisted Dying have demonstrated how the perceived religiosity of an argument, or even of the speaker himself, can be seen to invalidate a perspective - this will surely continue to be a problem if and when the House of Lords comes to benefit from broader religious representation. What type of argument will be capable of representing the views of the Muslim, Hindu or Jewish communities, if that is one genuine objective of a reform package, and how can these fail to be rooted in religious tradition? A number of prelates, and other peers, the most recent debate on Assisted Dying, felt obliged to respond specifically to criticisms along these lines:

> I, too, am concerned that there has been a tendency in wider debates to neutralise arguments of religious people on the grounds that they are religious arguments. I know that not absolutely all religious people oppose the Bill, but I also know that many people who would not associate themselves with any of the faith communities also oppose it. We all have ideologies, and proponents of the Bill in the House would be unwise to marginalise the views that come from these Benches and elsewhere because of who we are, as what we do day by day places us in contact with many, many other people.[66]

For some this would raise the question of what, if anything, the Lords Spiritual contributed to House of Lords' debates which could not have been delivered with greater authority and insight by the Lords' Temporal. Even where a view from a religious community is required, it need not come from a specifically religious bench. The answer to this will, for many, determine whether they consider the continued presence of the bishops in the House of Lords to be a unique opportunity which sees the socio-political issues at the heart of British life considered in the light of the wisdom of the Christian tradition, or an unfortunate fact of history which no one has had the time or inclination to undo.

chapter 4 - references

61 G Ecclestone, *The Church of England and Politics*, p. 51
62 F Bown, "Influencing the House of Lords: the Role of the Lords Spiritual, 1979-1987", *Political Studies*, XLII (1994), p. 117
63 John B Taylor in an interview with the author, 29 July 2002
64 Lords Hansard, 15 December 2004
65 Nick Spencer, "*Doing God*": *A Future for Faith in the Public Square*, p. 65 (Theos 2006)
66 Bishop of Portsmouth, Lords Hansard, 12 May 2006, col. 1226

5 coming off the bench

Our overview of the bishops' conduct over recent years has painted a complex picture of a Bench of Bishops whose contribution seems fluid over time and very much dependent on the proclivities (and the diocesan diary) of the individual. There is a perception, both inside and outside the House, that bishops are well-meaning but ineffectual part-timers. Nevertheless, there does appear to be a trend of increased politicization. Bishops are attending more, voting more and speaking more than at any other time over the last 30 years. A further stage of House of Lords' reform would probably see the shape and nature of the religious representation in Parliament change, so what does the current system offer?

a critical contribution?

> [I]f we attend to the example of Jesus, his solace and encouragement was for the most part given to the weak and poor and marginalized. The powerful and the decision-makers tended to find him a disturbing and a disconcerting presence. Theology's public statements should probably reflect the same qualities.[67]

Over the past 20 years, the attitude of the Church of England towards the State has been overwhelmingly critical. The changing nature of the connection we call establishment, and theological developments within the Anglican community, have seen it toe-to-toe with governments of both political persuasions on a variety of issues. This has been carried into the Bench of Bishops. In a trend which continued under Blair, the bishops under Thatcher tended to vote against the government whip twice as many times as they voted in their support and, in divisions which resulted in a government defeat, they were ten times as likely to vote with those seeking to bring about a government defeat as with the government. Generally, however, the bishops' voting was effective only in registering opinions, rather than altering outcomes. This influence must be gleaned from less concrete measures.

> **There is a perception, both inside and outside the House, that bishops are well-meaning but ineffectual part-timers. Nevertheless, there does appear to be a trend of increased politicization.**

a significant contribution?

You see the worst thing that happened was, we'd have a bishops' meeting at Lambeth which would end at lunchtime and quite a lot of the chaps would come into the Lords in the afternoon... and they would be discussing salmon fishing. The next day, the very next day, all the bishops have gone back for their jobs and there would be an absolute cracker debate on some social service and there would be just the duty bishop there. "Whoa, you were all here for salmon fishing, why weren't you here today?"[68]

The episcopal contribution is blighted by a series of obstacles, and in the past it has not been sufficiently considerable nor consistent to wield direct influence in the House. However, in recent years their contribution is becoming statistically more impressive, if not more effective. They very rarely change the outcome of a division through their numbers, but they have the potential to win hearts and minds. They probably remain "visitors rather than contributors",[69] but the trend is towards more attendance, more voting and more speech-making.

In view of the real obstacles that the bishops face in playing a full part in the House of Lords, their record is admirable. The bishops are, first and foremost, Anglican pastoral-managers with a full load of ecclesiastical responsibilities with which to contend. The procedures of the House (not least the emphasis on evening sittings)[70] militate against fitting attendance and speaking at the House into a busy diary. The reflections of former bishops tend to emphasize the hindering effect of these obstacles:

> [Y]ou see the trouble is everything is last minute, you don't know what's coming up for next week. People used to say, "so how disgraceful that only five of the bishops were there to vote", but what do you think I'm going to do? I've got a year's diary ahead of me already booked for the next year as it were. I was at this church this night, do I say to them when I've been booked for a year to go to their 150th anniversary that "sorry, I've got to go down and vote at the House?"[71]

> I was in Birmingham, you know it took two and a half hours by the time you left home to get into the House and it was very difficult to attend the House at all because my diary was made up one year ahead and the business with the House is made up one month ahead and you can't just cancel things simply, "Oh, I'm terribly sorry I can't, I'm in the House of Lords..." And so finding time to lobby that was out of the question really.[72]

> I always used to say that if 12 months ahead you said you would go to St Agatha's in the Mud, then to St Agatha's in the Mud you must go.[73]

> [Y]ou tried every excuse to get off a bit early because you'd got to get back for something or another or if you knew very well there were a pile of problems waiting on your desk needing to be dealt with.[74]

An admirable and improving record is not, however, the same as an effective record. At present, the bishops are required to work around these obstacles, as all peers with professional demands on their time must. However, if the bishops are to serve both Church and Parliament effectively, and if the House of Lords represents a genuine opportunity for the Church of England to bring authoritative, non-coercive counsel,[75] more needs to be done to remove these obstacles so that there is no longer a ceiling on the extent to which the bishops can contribute.

an efficient contribution?

The episcopal contribution to the House of Lords tends to be inefficient, the bulk of the bishops' voting and speech-making being undertaken, as it is, by a minority of those eligible to sit on the Bench of Bishops. A significant proportion (including those with *ex officio* seats) of the 26 bishops eligible to contribute to the House of Lords play no real part in its work. During the 1980s a group of just seven bishops cast 42% of the bishops' votes, and another group of seven bishops (including all but one of the vote-casting group of seven) made 65% of the bishops' speeches. Three-quarters of the speeches made from the Bench of Bishops were made by 17 individual bishops. While this is now a less marked feature of the bishops' contribution, it is still the case that in the last session for which we have figures 6 out of 25 contributed over half the speeches given. The sheer variety in the record of the attendance, voting and speech-making of each individual bishop is not a quirk of the duty bishop system, but an indication of what the prelate in question is capable of, and of what his other commitments allow.

Looking ahead to reform, this data adds weight to the case in support of Archbishop Fisher's suggestion that the number of bishops with seats in the Lords could be easily reduced, on the proviso that places should no longer be filled on the peculiar basis of seniority. Instead, selection should take account of the individual personality, experience, expertise and priorities of the individuals within the available pool of bishops. In the context of a reduction in the number of places for the Church of England bishops to 16, this would ensure that each of the places on the Bench of Bishops would be occupied by individual bishops committed, and able, to make use of the opportunity to contribute to the House. Equally, it would ensure that bishops ill-equipped to contribute to parliamentary life would be protected from expending their energies away from their calling within their diocese and the national structures of the Church. In view of the data presented on the voting and speech-making of the bishops, it is possible that the extent of the episcopal contribution could, to a degree, be maintained even if their numbers are forcibly reduced to 16. Put another way, it is a matter not just of how many, but of who. Indeed, if those bishops were given greater time to devote to their role at Westminster one could expect an increase in their voting and speech-making to take place. If not assisted by changes within Church structures, and an alteration to the appointment system, it is likely that the 16 bishops would struggle to maintain both the quantity and quality of the current contribution.

> ...more needs to be done to remove these obstacles so that there is no longer a ceiling on the extent to which the bishops can contribute.

a distinct contribution?

It can be argued that the bishops' contribution to the House of Lords is not sufficiently distinctive. The Lords Spiritual made use of facts and statistics to support their points on 197 occasions and academic and professional advice on 149 occasions. Meanwhile, reference was made to theological arguments on just 77 occasions, and explicit reference was made to the Bible during just 7% of their speeches. Only 1% of the episcopal contributions to the House of Lords explored biblical material in detail.

The most difficult question facing the religious element of a reformed second chamber will be what counts as a religiously distinctive yet publicly intelligible contribution. It is entirely appropriate that the bishops have brought a contribution to the House of Lords which communicates a competent understanding of the issues under discussion and that, in so doing, they have sought to depend on and refer to insights from science, political theory, sociology, economics, anthropology, and so on. Indeed, from a Christian perspective, reference to this body of knowledge is an intrinsic part of public theology; "hearing the Bible and observing human society must interact, creating what is often referred to as a hermeneutical spiral."[76] However, if the religious representatives of the future are forced by secularist voices into refusing even modest uses of theologically informed argument, they will be open to two particular accusations: firstly, that they will be unwitting contributors to, or willing victims of, the secularization of public life and, secondly, that their contributions could contain little which could not be presented to the House with authority by Lords Temporal. If they fail to provide the particular voice, reflecting religious belief in people's lives, then they will be acting outside of that which, according to Wakeham, is the raison d'être for their membership of the second chamber:[77]

> If what theology has to say in no significant way differs from what most people are saying anyway, theology and the church lose credibility; they should either have kept silent, or said something distinctive, rooted in their own convictions about God, human beings and fellowship.[78]

a future for the bishops?

> The presence of bishops in Parliament can point to an abiding validity of the Christian tradition to public doctrine and ethical norms ... Through the dioceses and parishes, through a small army of clergy and licensed lay ministers, through church schools and chaplaincies to many kinds of institutions, the Church of England has a vast constituency of pastoral contact which extends far beyond the core of committed churchgoers. The expression "national church" is not an anachronism.[79]

It is unlikely that the issue of religious representation will take a significant part in the political and parliamentary negotiations on House of Lords' reform, but a reformed second chamber which strikes the right balance between establishment, newly understood, and religious plurality, both in terms of Christian denominations and other faiths, could be one element of a settlement which sees marginalized religious communities being drawn into an open political conversation. There are a series of questions facing the Government, the Church of England and other faiths as they collectively embark on the next stage of reform.

The Church needs to consider more carefully how it can capitalize on this opportunity, and faith communities - if and when they get to the table - can learn from Anglican failures and successes. Donald Shell argues for the potential of the bishops to have an impact through their speeches to the House:

> Given the large cross-bench element and the independent-mindedness of peers generally, individual speeches can sway votes in the Lords, and the contributions made by bishops in general have an impact out of proportion to their numerical strength.[80]

John B Taylor describes his personal experience of the same sense of welcome and respect at the House of Lords:

> By and large they [Lords Temporal] very much appreciated what the bishop had to say. Because the bishops usually spoke sense. Because the bishop didn't speak with a party political card and steered very often through an argument and raised an issue that needed to be raised but was not a party-political ding-dong battle. I remember one saying to me: "In my opinion a bishop ought to speak in every debate". That was one of the younger ones.[81]

> *The Church needs to consider more carefully how it can capitalize on this opportunity, and faith communities - if and when they get to the table - can learn from Anglican failures and successes.*

The bishops also have an opportunity to influence the life of the nation through informal lobbying and friendship at Westminster. To the mind of Michael Baughen "[t]he main exchanges of value were not in the Chamber, they were outside the Chamber".[82] Lord Longford points to the bishops' failure to get involved in the informal lobbying and manoeuvring which takes place in the corridors, bars and restaurants of the Palace of Westminster ("perfectly respectable features of political life") as crucial to understanding their lack of influence in the House.[83] Asked whether he spent time off the floor of the House building informal relationships with decision-makers, John B Taylor gave a simple reply: "There wasn't time for it".[84] Hugh Montefiore responded in the same manner: "...one didn't have time".[85] If they are to become effective, the one thing the Lords Spiritual need is more time, both on and off the floor of the House, to make speeches, to vote, to do research and preparation, and most importantly to simply be present at the Palace of Westminster in order to engage informally with policy-makers.

Even outside the prospect of further reform, a case exists for the Church of England to undertake a review of its approach to episcopal parliamentary involvement in order to overcome those obstacles which hinder it from being a significant and influential voice in the House of Lords. Such a review would do well to listen to aspects of the proposal which Archbishop Geoffrey Fisher made to Prime Minister Clement Attlee in 1949 (which has received endorsement more recently from Trevor Beeson).[86] Edward Carpenter outlines Fisher's proposals in detail:

> The upshot of these consultations was a letter to the Prime Minister from the Archbishop in which he confirmed that those he had consulted were in general agreement with the proposals in respect of a reformed House of Lords so far as bishops were concerned. They approved that: (1) the two Archbishops, together with the bishops of London, Durham and Winchester should without question, retain their seats *ex officio*; (2) five other diocesan bishops should sit in the Lords; (3) these should not have their place in the Upper House merely on the grounds of seniority, but in terms of the likelihood of their making a useful contribution. Amongst these there should be younger bishops.[87]

Whether the number of Lords Spiritual was reduced to 10 or to 16, Fisher's suggestions make considerable sense if they are combined with the decision to release those bishops with seats in the House from a greater number of their diocesan responsibilities, specifically through the appointment of additional suffragans to serve the diocese. John B Taylor's response to this suggestion sets it in the context of the present role of suffragans and the value placed by the diocese itself on its bishop's wider ministry:

> You do leave others to run the diocese. A diocesan bishop is there to lead the diocese, someone else can run the diocese. There are expectations on you being present at this, that and the other. And you want to because you are very much the father of the family and you don't want to be out too frequently. But it has to be said that the diocese usually recognizes that they get back in benefits what they lose in time. Because you are bringing something back into your diocese from your contribution outside there in the world. And when they hear what you're doing they're glad that their man is involved. Very, very few dioceses resent the time that bishops spend in the House of Lords, or episcopal meetings or Church bodies, because they know very well that they are privileged to have a wider insight when they are talking with their bishops.[88]

There is a question of the total severance of the link between the Lord Spiritual and the diocese, which many believe would be unlikely to benefit the bishops' contribution to the House. It was considered by the Church of England's submission to the Wakeham Commission, and the Wakeham Commission itself found it to be crucial to the value of the bishops' contribution to the House of Lords[89] and analysis of the content of the bishops' speeches to the House indicates that they used arguments based on their diocesan and vocational experience more than any other.

a future for religious representation?

In the light of the evidence, and the likely reduction of the number of places available for Church of England bishops in a fully reformed second chamber, a considerable case exists for an evolution in the approach to religious representation in the House of Lords. Such an evolution must take into account the obstacles which at present hinder the Church of England bishops from bringing a significant moral and spiritual contribution to the debates of the House of Lords and to the life of its restaurants, bars, offices and corridors.

If there is a concern that the Church will lose influence in the Lords because of a reduction in its numerical representation, we would do well to remember that the numerical force of the episcopal contribution in voting is virtually never significant.[90] Indeed, in the past bishops have disavowed a view of their own role which sees them turning out in force to change the outcome of a vote, preferring to see the vote as a kind of Christian witness. Both the Church of England and those steering reform should also consider the merits of a more radical approach. Could the House of Lords be better served by 5 or 6 "working" bishops? The price would be the stretching of the link between the local community and the prelate, and the sacrificing of the breadth of the bishops' contribution. From the perspective of the Church of England, there have been enough examples of bishops who make a strong impact on public and political issues, but who do not regularly attend the House of Lords, for it not to be a necessary part of the public function of the bishops. The House would nonetheless benefit from a daily, consistent contribution from the Bench of Bishops within the context of a broader religious representation.

> **The wider responsibilities of a bishop remain the most significant block to consistent and greater involvement in the House of Lords.**

The wider responsibilities of a bishop remain the most significant block to consistent and greater involvement in the House of Lords. In either scenario those bishops who do serve on the Bench of Bishops could, through the appointment of additional suffragan bishops, be released from a greater number of their diocesan responsibilities so that they are able to play a more consistent and considerable part in the life of the second chamber. As we look to wider religious representation, different faith communities should consider who, within their ranks, would be best placed to make a similar significant contribution to the business of the House and how they could be released from wider responsibilities.

The selection of religious representatives to sit in the second chamber need not, as with the current Church of England system, be based on seniority. Rather, attention could be given to the particular personality, experience, expertise and priorities of individuals within the available pool of individuals. This could ensure that seats in the House are occupied by individuals willing and able to contribute to the second chamber. In view of the Wakeham Commission recommendations, this could be one role of the Appointments Commission.

Those serving as religious representatives in a reformed second chamber should be encouraged to consider how they can bring a more distinct moral and spiritual contribution to the House of Lords. In this context, particular attention needs to be given to considering what role the religious texts like the Bible can play in an open public discourse, and how theological perspectives can both remain part of their contribution, while not marginalizing their work. Religious representatives will need to live in the tension between meeting a bar of acceptable public reason and honouring their own traditions. A new understanding of the Church of England's establishment has seen it abandon its sectional interest and, certainly in the House of Lords, the bishops have become advocates for the religious communities at large, and a symbolic reminder of the spiritual and moral needs of people in general. Religious representatives from other faiths should ideally adopt the same *modus operandi*.

chapter 5 - references

67 DB Forrester, *Beliefs, Values and Policies*, p. 62-63
68 David Say in an interview with the author, 29 May 2002
69 Lord Orr-Ewing cited by F Bown, "Influencing the House of Lords: the Role of the Lords Spiritual, 1979-1987", *Political Studies*, XLII (1994), p. 106
70 Just 24% of the bishops' speeches were delivered during the five hours of the evening period as opposed to 70% during the two and a half hours of the afternoon period.
71 Michael Baughen in an interview with the author, 21 May 2002
72 Hugh Montefiore in an interview with the author, 21 May 2002
73 David Say in an interview with the author, 29 May 2002
74 John B Taylor in an interview with the author, 29 July 2002
75 Oliver O'Donovan, *Resurrection and the Moral Order*, p. 171
76 Jubilee Policy Group, *Political Christians in a Plural Society*, p. 30
77 Royal Commission on the Reform of the House of Lords, *A House for the Future*, Command Paper 4534, p. 151 (paragraph 15.5)
78 DB Forrester, *Beliefs, Values and Policies*, p. 81. See also Lee & Stanford who argue that "…it is precisely the theological input that the Church should be offering, whatever the topic on the table, for faith and the interpretation of Christian teaching is the church's distinctive contribution". S Lee & P Stanford, *Believing Bishops*, p. 31-32
79 Bishop of Durham, Lords Hansard, 7 March 2000, col. 932
80 D Shell, *The House of Lords*, p. 55
81 John B Taylor in an interview with the author 29 July 2002
82 Michael Baughen in an interview with the author, 21 May 2002
83 F Longford, *The Bishops*, p. 116
84 John B Taylor in an interview with the author, 29 July 2002
85 Hugh Montefiore in an interview with the author, 21 May 2002
86 T Beeson, *The Bishops*, p. 65
87 E Carpenter, *Archbishop Fisher*, p. 396
88 John B Taylor in an interview with the author, 29 July 2002
89 Archbishops' Council, *The Role of the Bishops in the Second Chamber*, p. 6-7; Royal Commission on the Reform of the House of Lords, *A House for the Future*, Command Paper 4534, p. 158
90 The largest vote in recent years was 14, this on a Private Members' Bill, and eventually immaterial to the result of the vote.

bibliography

Archbishops' Council	*The Role of the Bishops in the Second Chamber: A Submission by the Church of England*, GS Misc. 558 (London: Church House Publishing, 1999)
	Comments from the Church of England on the Government's White Paper (Unpublished: January 2002)
Archbishop of Canterbury's Commission on Church and State	*Church and State* 'The Chadwick Report' (London: Church House Publishing, 1970)
Avis, P	*Church, State and Establishment* (London: SPCK, 2001)
	The Anglican Understanding of the Church: An Introduction (London: SPCK, 2000)
Badham, P. (ed.)	*Religion, State and Society in Modern Britain* (Lampeter: Edwin Mellen Press, 1989)
Baldwin, NDJ & Shell, DR	*Second Chambers* (London: Frank Cass, 2001)
Beeson, T	*The Bishops* (London: SCM Press, 2002)
Bown, F	"Influencing the House of Lords: the Role of the Lords Spiritual 1979-1987", *Political Studies*, XLII (1994), pp. 105-119
	"The Defeat of the Shops Bill", M. Rush (ed.), *Parliament and Pressure Politics* (Oxford: Oxford University Press, 1990), pp. 213-233
Carpenter, E	*Archbishop Fisher: His Life and Times* (Norwich: The Canterbury Press, 1991)
Chadwick, O	*Michael Ramsey: A Life* (Oxford: Clarendon Press, 1990)
Clark, H	*The Church Under Thatcher* (London: SPCK, 1993)
Cornwell, P	"The Church of England and the State: Changing Constitutional Links in Historical Perspective," GH Moyser (ed.), *Church and Politics Today: The Role of the Church of England in Contemporary Politics* (Edinburgh: T & T Clark, 1985), pp. 33-54
Davie, G	*Religion in Britain Since 1945: Believing Without Belonging* (Oxford: Blackwell, 1994)
Ecclestone, G	*The Church of England and Politics* (London: Church House Publishing, 1981)
Forrester, D.B	*Beliefs, Values and Policies* (Oxford: Clarendon Press, 1989)
Government White Paper	*Modernising Parliament: The Reform of the House of Lords*, Cm 4183 (London: The Stationery Office, January 1999)
	The House of Lords: Completing the Reform, Cm 5291 (London: The Stationery Office, November 2001)

Harries, R.	"Why we need faith in the Lords", *Church Times* 24 May 2002
Hastings, A	*Robert Runcie* (London: Mowbray, 1991)
	Church and State: The English Experience (Exeter: University of Exeter Press, 1991)
Haynes, J	*Religion in Global Politics* (London: Longman, 1998)
Jubilee Policy Group	*Political Christians in a Plural Society: A New Strategy for a Biblical Contribution* (Cambridge: The Jubilee Policy Group, 1994)
Lee, S & Stanford, P	*Believing Bishops* (London: Faber & Faber, 1990)
Longford, F	*The Bishops: A Study of Leaders in the Church Today* (London: Sodgwick & Jackson, 1986)
Medhurst, KN & Moyser, GH	*Church and Politics in a Secular Age* (Oxford: Clarendon Press, 1988)
	"Lambeth Palace, the Bishops and Politics", in GH Moyser (ed.), *Church and Politics Today: The Role of the Church of England in Contemporary Politics* (Edinburgh: T & T Clark, 1985), pp. 75-106
	"From Princes to Pastors: The Changing Position of the Anglican Episcopate in English Society and Politics", *West European Politics*, Vol. 5, No. 2 (April 1982), pp. 172-91
Modood, T	"Ethno-religious minorities, Secularism and the British State", *British Political Quarterly* (1994), pp. 61-65
Moyser, GH (ed.),	*Church and Politics Today: The Role of the Church of England in Contemporary Politics* (Edinburgh: T & T Clark, 1985)
Moyser, GH	"The Church of England and Politics: Patterns and Trends", GH Moyser (ed.), *Church and Politics Today: The Role of the Church of England in Contemporary Politics* (Edinburgh: T & T Clark, 1985), pp. 1-24
Nash, ML	"The Leaven in the Lump: Bishops in the House of Lords", *Contemporary Review*, 1999
O'Donovan, O	*Resurrection and the Moral Order: An Outline for Evangelical Ethics* (Leicester: IVP, 1986)
Rivers, J	"Disestablishment and the Church of England", M. Schluter (ed.), *Christianity in a Changing World: Biblical Insights on Contemporary Issues* (London: Marshall Pickering, 2000), pp. 63-80

Rogers, D	*Politics, Prayer and Parliament* (London: Continuum, 2000)
Royal Commission on the House of Lords	*A House for the Future*, Command Paper 4534 House Reform of the (London: Stationery Office, January 2000)
Russell, M and Sciara, M	"Why does the Government get defeated in the House of Lords?" - Paper to 2006 PSA Conference (5 April 2006) and available at **www.ucl.ac.uk/constitution-unit**
Shell, D.R	*The House of Lords* (London: Harvester Wheatsheaf, 1992)
Sheppard, D.S	*Steps Along Hope Street: My Life in Cricket, the Church and the Inner City* (London, Hodder and Stoughton, 2002)
Spencer, N	*Doing God: A Future for Faith in the Public Square* (Theos, 2006)
Whale, J	*The Anglican Church Today: The Future of Anglicanism* (Oxford: Mowbray, 1988)

Open access. Some rights reserved
Policy Statement

This work is licensed under the Creative Commons
Attribution - Noncommercial - No Derivative Works 2.5 Licence (the "Licence").
To view a copy of this Licence:

- visit http://creativecommons.org/licenses/by-nc-nd/2.5/
- or send a letter to Creative Commons, 543 Howard Street, 5th Floor, San Francisco, California, 94105, USA.

creative commons

creativecommons.org

As the publisher of this work, Theos has an open access policy that enables anyone to access our content electronically without charge.

Please read and consider the terms and conditions set out in the Licence, details of which can be obtained via the Internet or post at the relevant addresses set out above.

Users are welcome to download, save, perform, or distribute this work electronically or in any other format, including in foreign language translation, without written permission subject to the conditions set out in the Licence. The following are some of the conditions imposed by the Licence:

- Theos and the author(s) are credited;
- Theos's website address (www.theosthinktank.co.uk) is published together with a copy of this Policy Statement in a prominent position;
- the text is not altered and is used in full (the use of extracts under existing fair usage rights is not affected by this condition);
- the work is not resold; and
- a copy of the work or link to use on-line is sent to the address below for our archive.

Theos
Licence Department
34 Buckingham Palace Road
London
SW1W 0RE
United Kingdom

hello@theosthinktank.co.uk

Please contact us if you would like permission to use this work for purposes outside of the scope of the Licence.

creative commons
COMMONS DEED

Attribution-NonCommercial-NoDerivs 2.5

You are free:

- to copy, distribute, display, and perform the work

Under the following conditions:

Attribution. You must attribute the work in the manner specified by the author or licensor.

Noncommercial. You may not use this work for commercial purposes.

No Derivative Works. You may not alter, transform, or build upon this work.

- For any reuse or distribution, you must make clear to others the license terms of this work.
- Any of these conditions can be waived if you get permission from the copyright holder.

Your fair use and other rights are in no way affected by the above.